Revealed Love

Barbara Bolivar

Print information available on the last page

Rev. date: 04/25/2019

To order additional copies of this book, contact:
Xlibris
1-888-795-4274
www.Xlibris.com
Orders@Xlibris.com

Dedicated To God, friends, family and specially my grandsons Angel and Elon Serrano. I love you all to the moon and back:)

Once upon a time, Mia met Jesus.
Right away, she loved Him so much!

She didn't know God already had a plan for her, before she was born. Soon she discovered she was here on earth to share God's love with people all over the world.

Mia began to take small steps of faith and began her journey to Nicaragua, the Philippines and Mexico. She loved the nations, the people, and the culture.

Mexico

Nicaragua

Philippines

When Mia was around children and their families, she felt joy, peace, and knew God was stirring her heart for people all over the world.

She began to think, "How can I share the love of Jesus with others all over the world?"

While she was in the Philippines finishing a mission trip, Mia heard Jesus's voice say, "Now Peru." Mia soon discovered Jesus was telling her to go to the land where she was born.

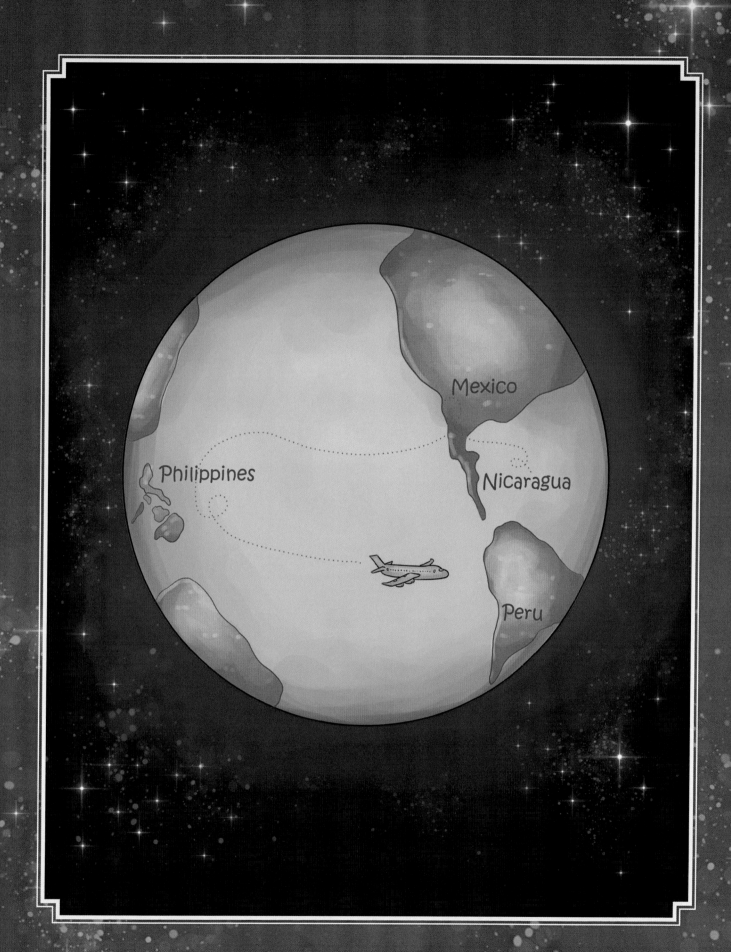

But her heart felt very sad because this meant she would leave her children, her grandchildren, family and friends to share God's love with others.

Mia began to pray to Jesus. She knew that Jesus would take care of her family and friends. As she read the Bible and prayed, she felt love, joy, and peace.

Mia knows that no matter how far away she is from her family and friends, their love would always hold them together. Mia decided to obey Jesus.

Jesus speaks, and Mia follows.

Have you ever invited Jesus into your heart?

You can just pray, "Jesus, come into my heart; forgive me of all my sins. Be the King of my heart and show me how to obey you. Amen."

Romans 10: 9

Printed in the United States
By Bookmasters

The way the book came along was through a vision I received from the Lord. I believe I was led by the Holy Spirit when I wrote this book. I was at a point in my life where I knew I was being led by God to go on mission trips for an extended period, which would require me to step away from my children and grandchildren longer than I am used to. The agony I felt in my heart knowing I will be apart from my family was the sacrifice I will be paying to be obedient to God's purpose in my life. The vision God gave me was of me reading a book to my grandchildren. Writing a book was never a dream of mine, but God works in mysterious ways. And therefore, I believed in the impossible and wrote my first book.

Barbara Bolivar is a woman of faith. The purpose of her life is to share the love of God all over the world as a missionary. She seeks to go to places where there is no light, and no hope to the orphans and present Jesus. In her walk of faith, God has revealed to her that no one is left behind. She strives to build up children into the Kingdom of God through His word. She hungers to see His kingdom coming together as one and turning this world upside down for the better.

Xlibris

ISBN 978-1-7960-3042-6
51599

9 781796 030426

THE PLAN
IL PROGETTO

A bilingual story English and Italian about Hope

Una storia bilingue in Inglese e italiano sulla Speranza

Written by / Scritta da
Francesca Follone-Montgomery, ofs

Illustrated by/ illustrata da
Gennel Marie Sollano